T0045006

Eensy Weensy Spider

& Other Nursery Rhyme Favorites

Contents

ISBN 978-0-634-00082-9

HAL•LEONARD®
CORPORATION

7777 W. BLUEMOUND RD. P.O. BOX 13819 MILWAUKEE, WI 53213

Visit Hal Leonard Online at
www.halleonard.com

Eensy, Weensy Spider

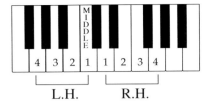

L.H.　　R.H.

Traditional

Creep and crawl

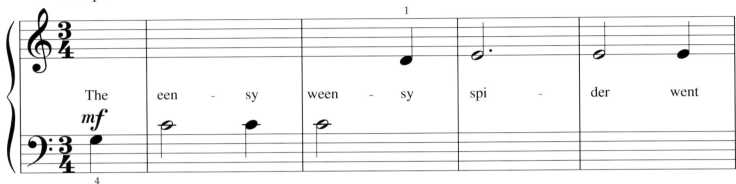

The een - sy ween - sy spi - der went

mf

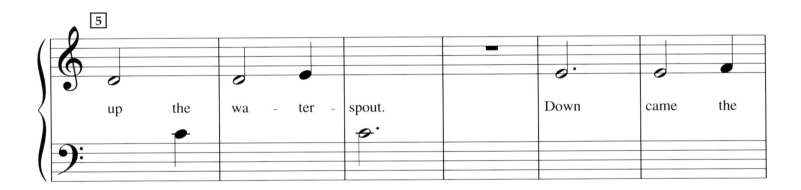

up the wa - ter - spout. Down came the

Duet Part (Student plays one octave higher than written.)

Creep and crawl

mf

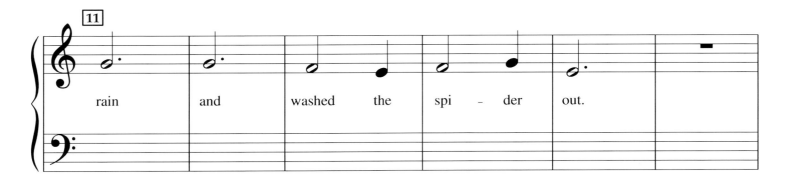

rain   and   washed   the   spi - der   out.

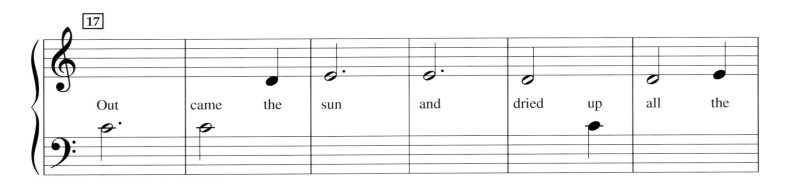

Out   came   the   sun   and   dried   up   all   the

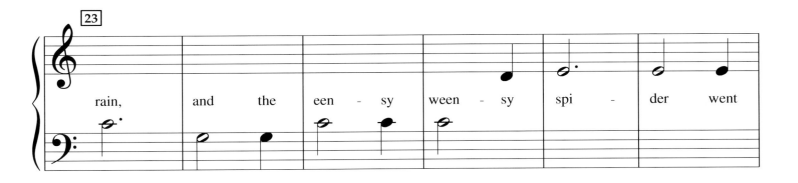

rain,   and   the   een - sy   ween - sy   spi - der   went

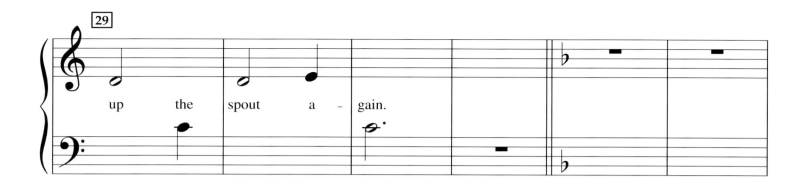

up   the   spout   a   –   gain.

Let your right hand
walk like a spider!

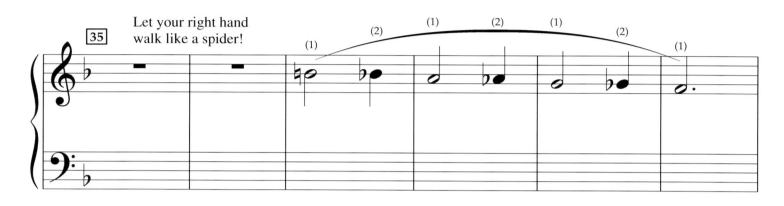

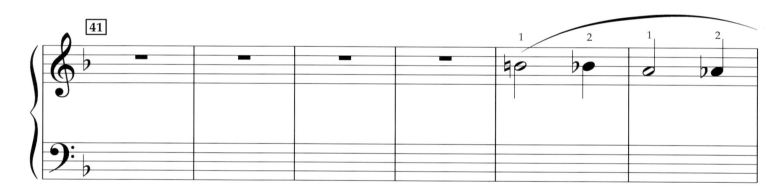

sim.

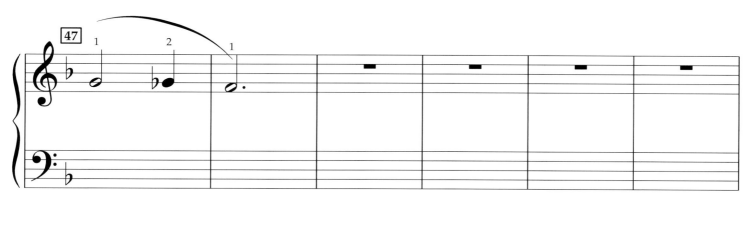

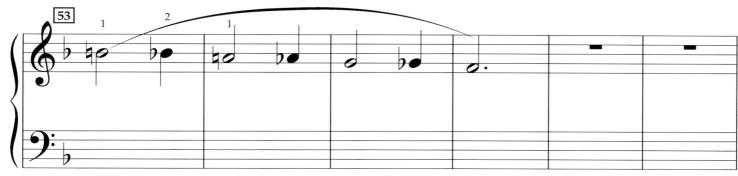

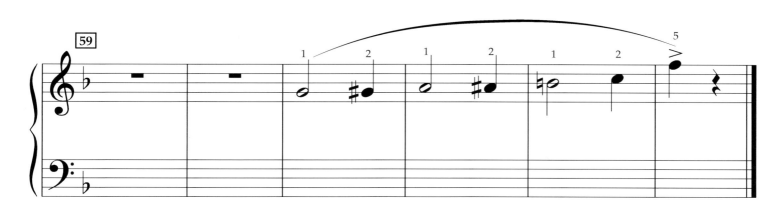

Hickory, Dickory, Dock

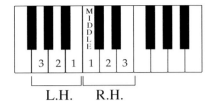

Moderately fast

Traditional

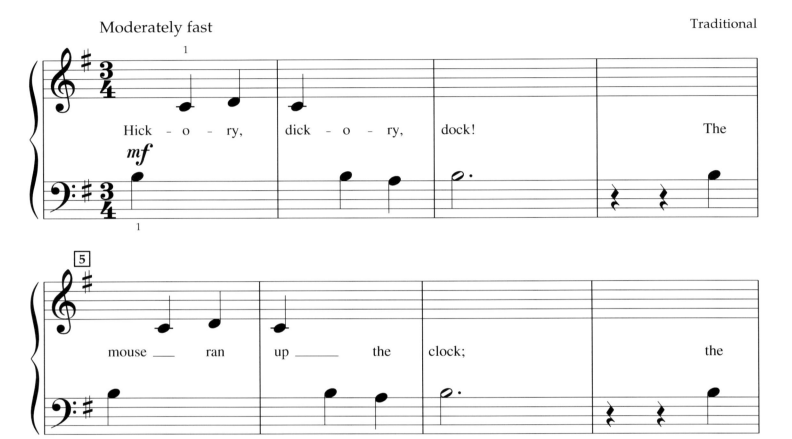

Hick - o - ry, dick - o - ry, dock! The
mouse ___ ran up ___ the clock; the

Duet Part (Student plays one octave higher than written.)

Moderately fast

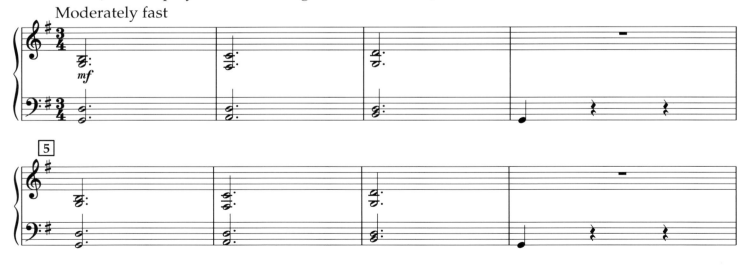

clock   struck   one,   and   down   he   run.

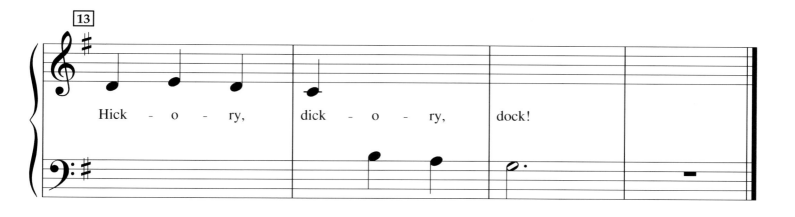

Hick – o – ry,   dick – o – ry,   dock!

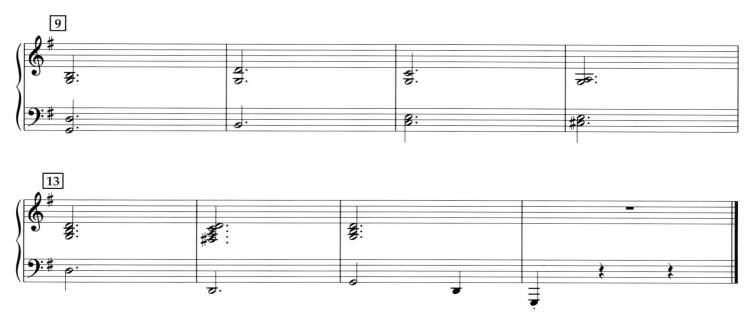

umpty Dum ty

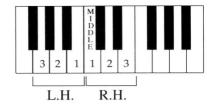

Moderately fast

Traditional

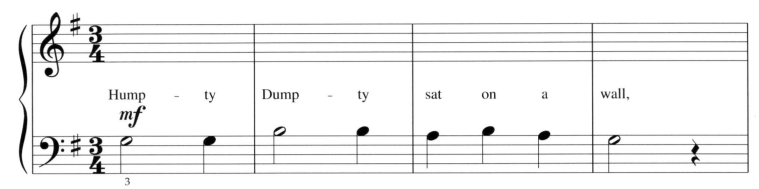

Hump – ty Dump – ty sat on a wall,

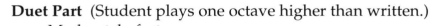

Hump – ty Dump – ty had a great fall.

Duet Part (Student plays one octave higher than written.)

Moderately fast

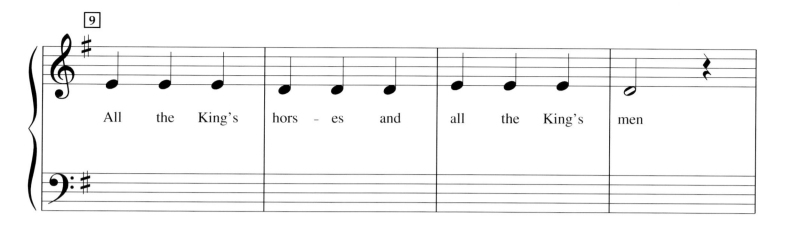

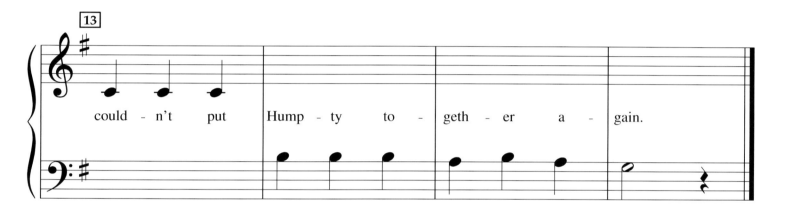

Hush, Little Baby

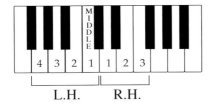

Carolina Folk Lullaby

Gently

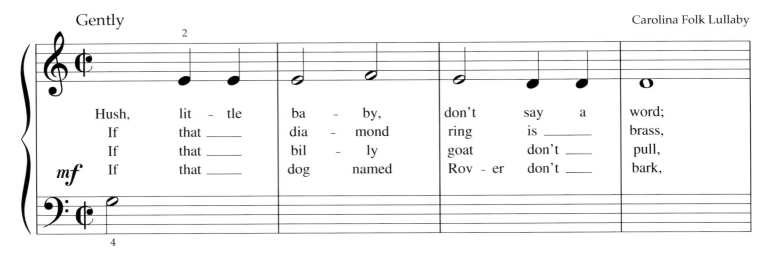

Hush, lit – tle ba – by, don't say a word;
If that _____ dia – mond ring is _____ brass,
If that _____ bil – ly goat don't _____ pull,
If that _____ dog named Rov – er don't _____ bark,

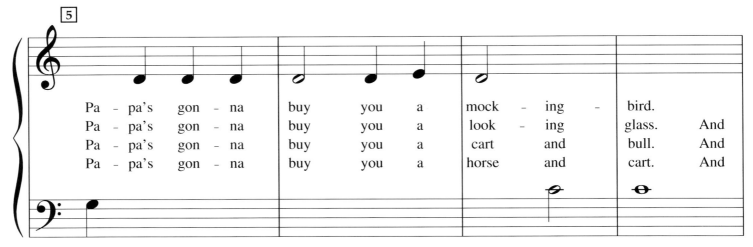

Pa – pa's gon – na buy you a mock – ing – bird.
Pa – pa's gon – na buy you a look – ing – glass. And
Pa – pa's gon – na buy you a cart and bull. And
Pa – pa's gon – na buy you a horse and cart. And

Duet Part (Student plays one octave higher than written.)

Gently

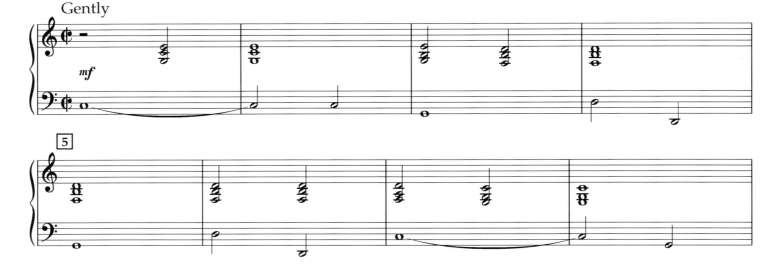

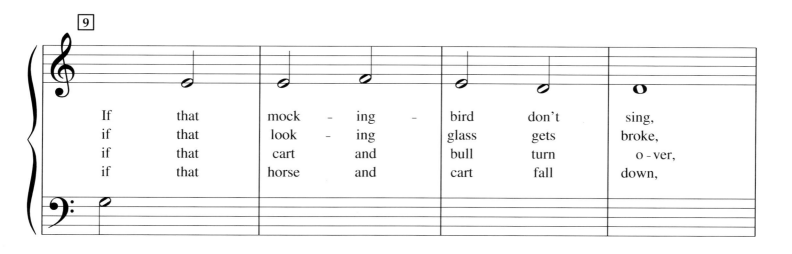

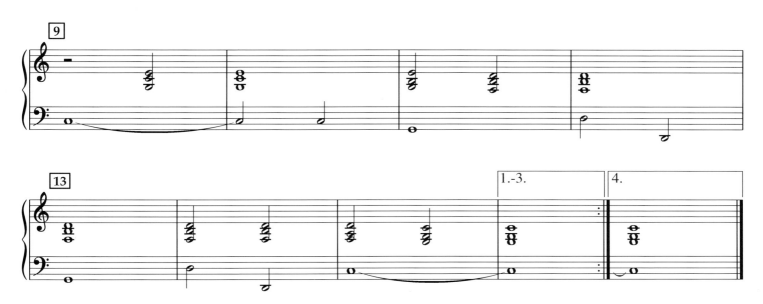

Jack and Jill

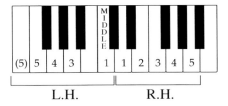

Brightly

Traditional

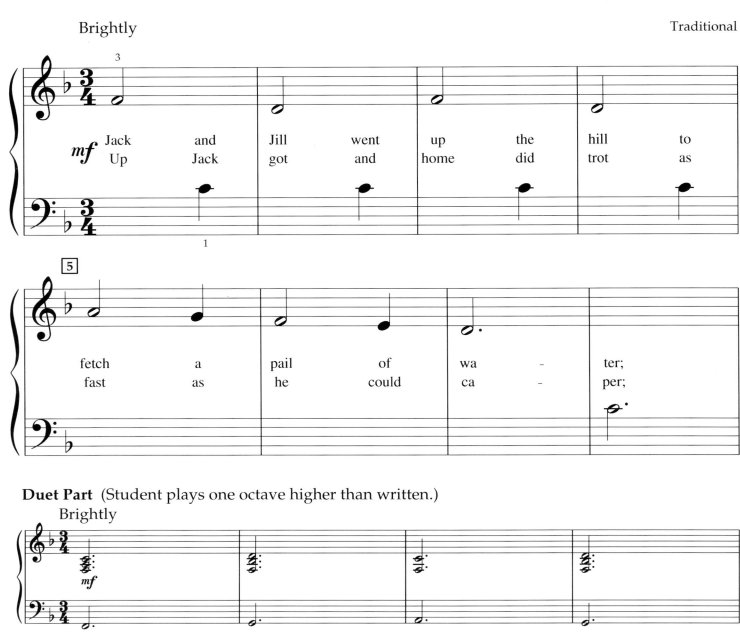

Jack   and   Jill   went   up   the   hill   to
Up   and   Jack   got   and   home   did   trot   as

fetch   a   pail   of   wa   -   ter;
fast   as   he   could   ca   -   per;

Duet Part (Student plays one octave higher than written.)

Brightly

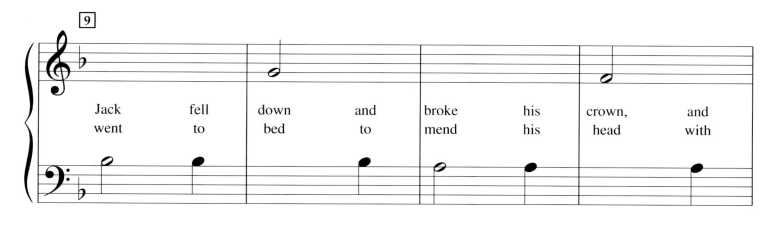

Jack   fell   down   and   broke   his   crown,   and
went   to   bed   to   mend   his   head   with

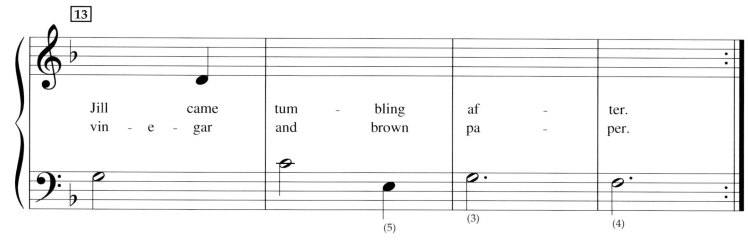

Jill   came   tum - bling   af -   ter.
vin - e - gar   and   brown   pa -   per.

(5)   (3)   (4)

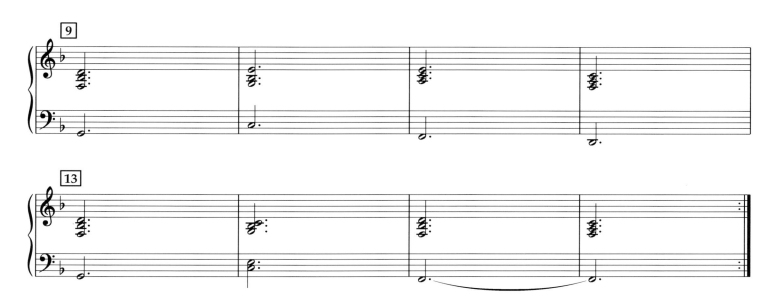

Little Jack Horner

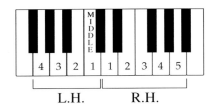

L.H.   R.H.

Moderately

Traditional

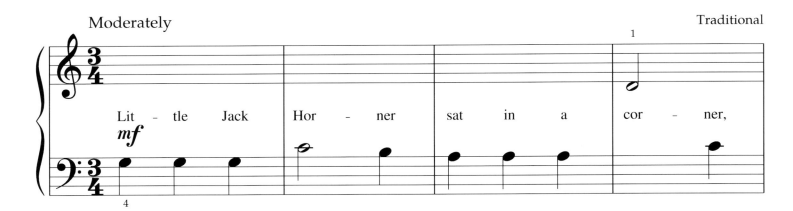

Lit - tle Jack Hor - ner sat in a cor - ner,

mf

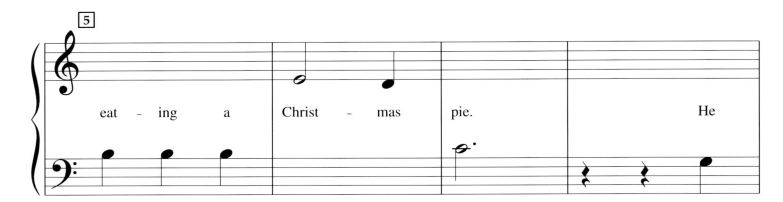

eat - ing a Christ - mas pie.   He

Duet Part (Student plays one octave higher than written.)

Moderately

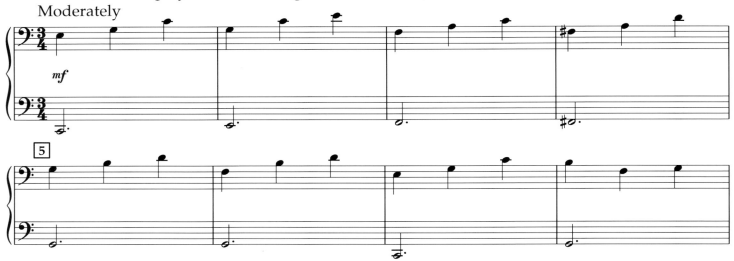

mf

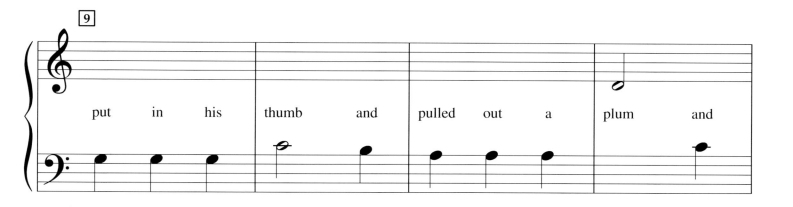

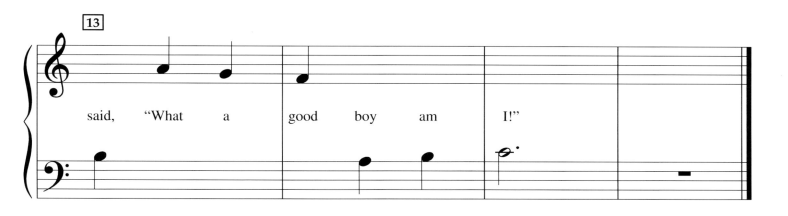

put in his thumb and pulled out a plum and

said, "What a good boy am I!"

15

Mary Ha a Little Lam

L.H.   R.H.

Words by Sarah Josepha Hale
Traditional Music

Lively

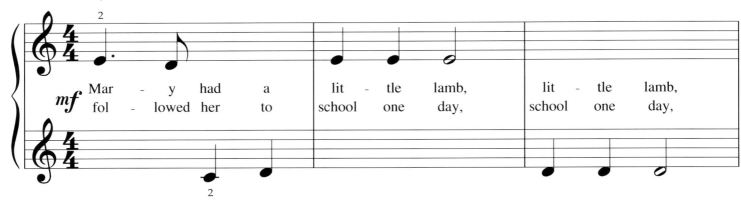

Mar - y had a   lit - tle lamb,   lit - tle lamb,
fol - lowed her to   school one day,   school one day,

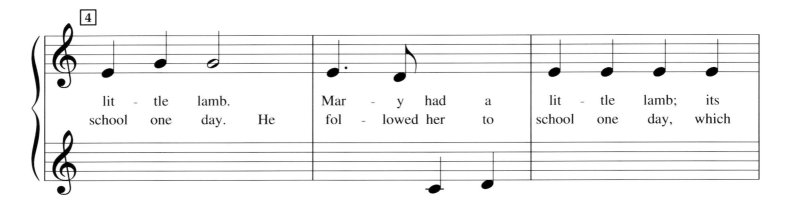

lit - tle lamb.   Mar - y had a   lit - tle lamb;   its
school one day. He   fol - lowed her to   school one day, which

Duet Part (Student plays two octaves higher than written.)

Lively

17

Old King Col

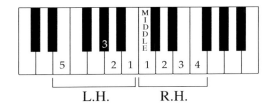

L.H.   R.H.

Moderately

Traditional

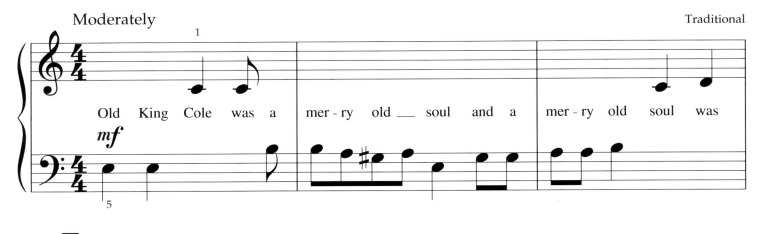

Old King Cole was a mer-ry old __ soul and a mer-ry old soul was

mf

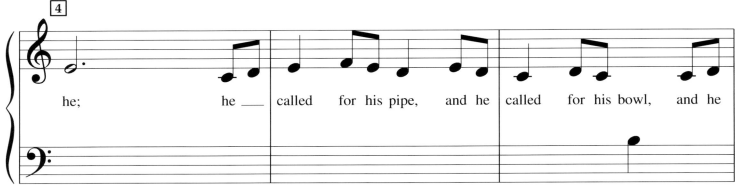

he;   he __ called for his pipe, and he called for his bowl, and he

Duet Part (Student plays one octave higher than written.)

Moderately

mf

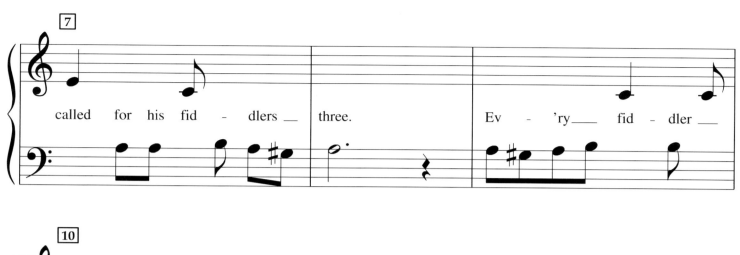

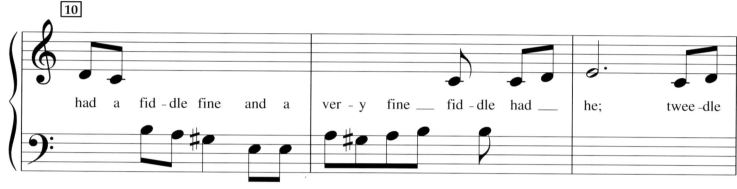

Peter, Peter, Pumpkin Eater

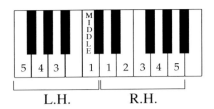

L.H.   R.H.

Moderately fast

Traditional

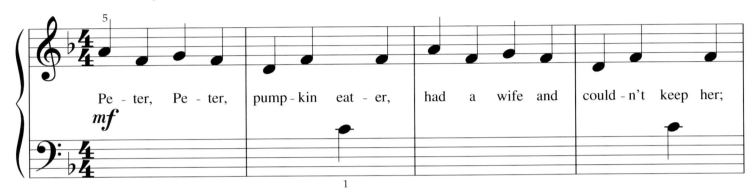

Pe - ter, Pe - ter, pump - kin eat - er, had a wife and could - n't keep her;

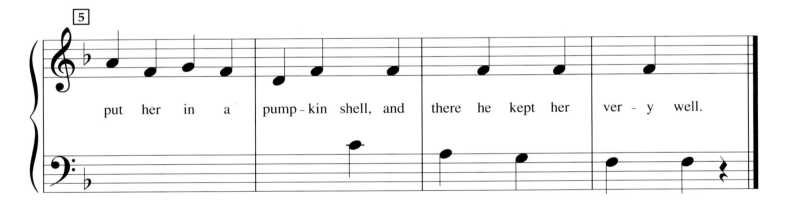

put her in a pump - kin shell, and there he kept her ver - y well.

Duet Part (Student plays one octave higher than written.)
Moderately fast

Tom, Tom, the Piper's Son

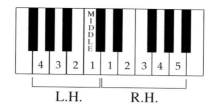

L.H.   R.H.

Moderately

Traditional

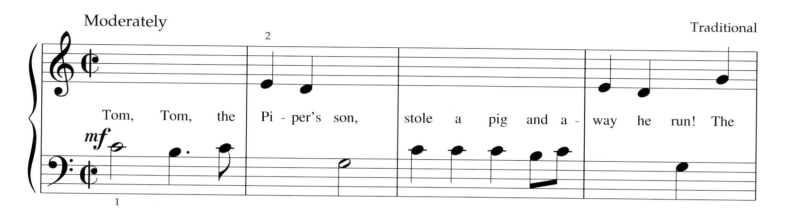

Tom, Tom, the   Pi - per's son,   stole a pig and a - way he run! The

mf

pig was eat and   Tom was beat and   Tom went cry - ing   down the street.

Duet Part (Student plays one octave higher than written.)

Moderately

mf

Pop Goes the Weasel

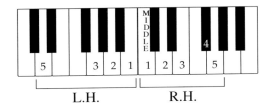

Lively

Traditional

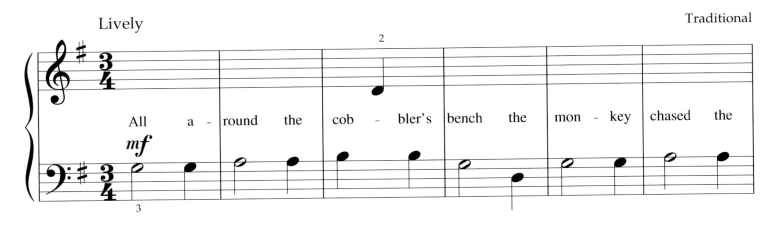

All a - round the cob - bler's bench the mon - key chased the

mf

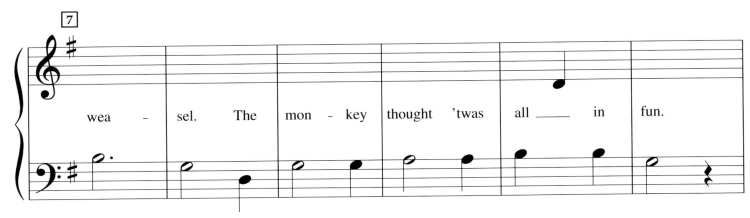

wea - sel. The mon - key thought 'twas all _____ in fun.

Duet Part (Student plays one octave higher than written.)

Lively

mf

PLAYING PIANO HAS NEVER BEEN EASIER!

5-Finger Piano Collections from Hal Leonard

BEATLES! BEATLES!

8 classics, including: A Hard Day's Night • Hey Jude • Love Me Do • P.S. I Love You • Ticket to Ride • Twist and Shout • Yellow Submarine • Yesterday.
00292061..$8.99

CHILDREN'S TV FAVORITES
Themes from 8 Hit Shows

Five-finger arrangements of the themes for: Barney • Bob the Builder • Thomas the Tank Engine • Dragon Tales • PB&J Otter • SpongeBob SquarePants • Rugrats • Dora the Explorer.
00311208..$7.95

CHURCH SONGS FOR KIDS

Features five-finger arrangements of 15 sacred favorites, including: Amazing Grace • The B-I-B-L-E • Down in My Heart • Fairest Lord Jesus • Hallelu, Hallelujah! • I'm in the Lord's Army • Jesus Loves Me • Kum Ba Yah • My God Is So Great, So Strong and So Mighty • Oh, How I Love Jesus • Praise Him, All Ye Little Children • Zacchaeus • and more.
00310613..$8.99

CLASSICAL FAVORITES – 2ND EDITION

Includes 12 beloved classical pieces from Bach, Bizet, Haydn, Grieg and other great composers: Bridal Chorus • Hallelujah! • He Shall Feed His Flock • Largo • Minuet in G • Morning • Rondeau • Surprise Symphony • To a Wild Rose • Toreador Song.
00310611..$7.95

DISNEY MOVIE FUN

8 classics, including: Beauty and the Beast • When You Wish Upon a Star • Whistle While You Work • and more.
00292067..$8.99

DISNEY TUNES

Includes: Can You Feel the Love Tonight? • Chim Chim Cher-ee • Go the Distance • It's a Small World • Supercalifragilisticexpialidocious • Under the Sea • You've Got a Friend in Me • Zero to Hero.
00310375..$8.99

SELECTIONS FROM DISNEY'S PRINCESS COLLECTION VOL. 1

7 songs sung by Disney heroines – with a full-color illustration of each! Includes: Colors of the Wind • A Dream Is a Wish Your Heart Makes • I Wonder • Just Around the Riverbend • Part of Your World • Something There • A Whole New World.
00310847 ....$8.99

EENSY WEENSY SPIDER & OTHER NURSERY RHYME FAVORITES

Includes 11 rhyming tunes kids love: Hickory Dickory Dock • Humpty Dumpty • Hush, Little Baby • Jack and Jill • Little Jack Horner • Mary Had a Little Lamb • Peter, Peter Pumpkin Eater • Pop Goes the Weasel • Tom, Tom, the Piper's Son • more.
00310465..$7.95

FIRST POP SONGS

Eight timeless pop classics are presented here in accessible arrangements: Candle in the Wind • Lean on Me • Moon River • Piano Man • Tears in Heaven • Unchained Melody • What a Wonderful World • Yellow Submarine.
00123296..$8.99

FROZEN
Music from the Motion Picture

Seven popular songs from *Frozen* are featured in single-note melody lines that stay in one position in this songbook. Songs include: Do You Want to Build a Snowman? • Fixer Upper • For the First Time in Forever • In Summer • Let It Go • Love Is an Open Door • Reindeer(s) Are Better Than People. Includes lyrics and beautifully-written accompaniments.
00130374..$10.99

POP HITS FOR FIVE-FINGER PIANO

8 hot hits that even beginners can play, including: Cups (When I'm Gone) • Home • I Won't Give Up • Love Story • Next to Me • Skyfall • What Makes You Beautiful • When I Was Your Man. These books also include optional duet parts for a teacher or parent to play that makes the student sound like a pro!
00123295..$8.99

THE SOUND OF MUSIC

8 big-note arrangements of popular songs from this perennial favorite musical, including: Climb Ev'ry Mountain • Do-Re-Mi • Edelweiss • The Lonely Goatherd • My Favorite Things • Sixteen Going on Seventeen • So Long, Farewell • The Sound of Music.
00310249..$9.99

SELECTIONS FROM *STAR WARS*
arr. Robert Schultz

Based on the fantastic series of *Star Wars* movies, these songs were carefully selected and arranged by Robert Schultz at the five finger level. Included in the folio are: Anakin's Theme • Augie's Great Municipal Band • Cantina Band • Duel of the Fates • The Imperial March • Luke and Leia • Princess Leia's Theme • Star Wars (Main Title) • Yoda's Theme.
00321903..$9.99

HAL•LEONARD®

www.halleonard.com